MINISCAPES

MINISCAPES

CREATE YOUR OWN TERRARIUM

⋘⟡⟡⟡⟡⟡⟡⟡⟡⟡⟡⋙ Clea Cregan ⋘⟡⟡⟡⟡⟡⟡⟡⟡⟡⟡⋙

hardie grant books

Contents

◇◇◇◇◇◇◇◇◇◇◇◇◇◇◇◇◇◇◇◇◇◇

◇◇◇◇◇◇◇◇◇◇◇◇◇◇◇◇◇◇◇◇◇◇

What is a Terrarium?

TER·RAR·I·UM

terre — earth • *ium* — with

Welcome to the wonderful world of terrariums. What exactly are these miniature biomes? A terrarium is a glass vessel filled with small plants, rocks, and soil. These tiny gardens mimic real landscapes. They bring nature inside and are the perfect green addition to any space. Terrarium gardening is low-maintenance and really easy. "But, I always kill plants!" I hear you say. Fear not, a terrarium is the perfect green companion for you.

I live in a big city and am very much an urban dweller. I spend a lot of my time staring at screens and admit that I'm pretty removed from nature. I have a few token houseplants dotted around but they are often droopy and always shrivel when I go on holiday. I've always termed myself a 'lazy gardener', absent-mindedly forgetting to feed and water my plants.

A bonsai bug had caught me earlier in life, but there were, sadly, many casualties. Bonsai are high maintenance and they did not match my 'relaxed' approach to gardening. But, browsing through a country thrift store about seven years ago, I stumbled upon a beautiful old book from 1975 about terrarium gardening. The pages were filled with photos of these captivating miniature environments – tiny little landscapes enclosed in glass.

The appeal of these gardens was not only their beauty, but their self-sufficient nature. The connection was instant! Soon, I was filling any glass vessel I could find with these little green worlds. I was scouring the internet, second-hand shops and markets for interesting glass shapes and quirky objects to put inside. I had caught the terrarium bug! Terrariums bring together my love of design, nature and anything 'mini'. I was hooked by the tactile nature of working with plants. Our house soon became over-flowing with terrariums and this is how my business Miniscapes was born. Before long, Miniscape worlds started appearing in shops, cafes, and offices around Melbourne.

The modern terrarium revival had begun and I was lucky enough to be a part of it.

In this book I am going to show you how to make your very own tiny garden. Like me, you do not need a green thumb to become a terrarium gardener. This book will guide you step-by-step through the process of creating your own beautiful living sculpture that can be enjoyed all year round, whatever the weather is like outside. We will cover the basics from soil and rocks, moss and tools, to growing and choosing your plants, containers and decorations. There are 16 projects to follow that show you how simple and diverse terrarium gardening can be. Before long you will be creating your own miniature green worlds and making the perfect 'green' gift that is so much more exciting than a bunch of flowers. I hope you will enjoy tiny gardening as much as I do.

Warning: terrarium gardening can be very addictive!

How a Terrarium Works

You may or may not remember from school science lessons the process of photosynthesis. If not, here's a quick refresher.

Plants create their energy from light, soil and air. Leaves take in carbon dioxide and sunlight, while water is absorbed through the plant's roots. This creates glucose, which the plant turns into energy. The plant then releases oxygen into the air.

In a closed terrarium, the glass absorbs light, which increases the internal temperature. This causes moisture to evaporate from the leaves, which creates condensation within the terrarium. Droplets, or fog, form on the glass walls, and as the water collects, the 'fog' starts to behave like clouds. The moisture then 'rains' back down onto the soil for the cycle to continue.

A closed terrarium can go for years without requiring extra water. It becomes its own mini ecosystem, as the moisture in the soil never evaporates and the air is constantly recycled. In this kind of stable microclimate, the plants will thrive.

In an open terrarium, respiration still occurs but moisture escapes more easily, so you need to water it regularly. Open terrariums are better suited to cacti, succulents and other like-minded plants that prefer air circulation and low humidity.

Remember, terrariums work best when LIGHT, WATER and HUMIDITY are correctly balanced.

GETTING STARTED

horticultural
charcoal

gravel

sphagnum moss

plants

The Basics

The foundations for a happy terrarium depend upon a few key factors. I find that sourcing all the materials is the most time consuming part; the actual planting is quite straightforward. Like any good recipe, you will need to have all the ingredients ready before you begin assembling, as they are all critical in the layers of your terrarium.

Location and container type
- Where you would like to put your terrarium.
- The amount of light available (this will dictate the types of plants you use).
- The size and shape of your container (how much headroom is there for the plants to grow?).
- Is your container open or closed?

Optional elements to personalise your terrarium
- Moss
- Figurines
- Rocks
- Driftwood
- Shells
- Crystals

Basic equipment
- A glass container
- Pebbles, gravel or rocks
- Activated or horticulture charcoal
- Potting mix
- Plants

preserved reindeer
moss, crystals
and driftwood

Planning

The best resource for planning your terrarium design is to observe how plants grow together in nature. Take a walk through a forest or visit your local botanical gardens. Notice how the combinations of different layers and textures work together. You want to mimic these landscapes in your terrarium.

The next step is to decide on a theme for your terrarium: forest, desert, carnivorous or air plant. Closed containers or those with small openings are ideal for forest biomes, whereas open containers are perfect for desert, carnivorous and air plant terrariums. The size and shape of your container will also dictate the number of plants you grow. In a small terrarium, one plant, a rock and some ground cover may be all that will fit. Larger containers may hold 3–5 plants, but make sure that you don't overcrowd your terrarium, as the plants will need room to grow.

Ideally, you should try and include:
◉ Ground cover
◉ One tall plant
◉ A couple of medium-sized plants.

When designing your terrarium, try arranging the plants in pots before planting or do a rough sketch of how you would like your landscape to look. Experiment with different levels of soil, adding terraces, hills and valleys – this will make your scene more interesting. I find that an odd number of plants looks best. Choose one plant to be the focal point and aim for a variety of heights, textures, colours and shapes in the foliage. Spin your container around and decide which side will be the front. Try and arrange the plants so that the larger plants are towards the middle or the back of your terrarium.

Containers

Any clear glass container can be made into a terrarium; the possibilities are endless!

On your travels, keep your eye out for interesting glass containers. You might find these in thrift stores, gift shops, florists, markets, garage sales, antique shops or online (Ebay and Etsy are great sources for finding interesting glassware). You might find the perfect glass vessel already in your kitchen – canisters, big jars or even glass salad bowls are all suitable.

I only make terrariums with clear glass containers, as coloured glass doesn't filter the full colour spectrum of light that the plants need to survive. Plastic containers will also work but plastic won't regulate the temperature as well.

Large pickling jars, science beakers, vases, carboys, apothecary jars, display cloches, candy jars, bowls, hurricane lanterns, fish bowls and aquariums are all potential containers for your terrarium.

The type of container you choose will dictate the style of terrarium you will create.

Containers must be washed thoroughly before use with hot soapy water. Rinse out any soap residue, remove any stickers or labels and allow to completely dry before you begin planting.

Closed containers that are sealed with a lid or have a small opening, are ideal for moisture-loving tropical plants and ferns.

Open bowls and dish terrariums are great for succulents and air plants, and will allow you a wider selection of plants. These plants won't survive in a closed terrarium.

You can use tropical plants and ferns in open terrariums but they will require more watering.

Bottle gardens are terrariums made in narrow-necked containers, but these can be tricky to plant. You will need specialised slender tools, as the small opening will limit the plants that will fit. Maintaining and cleaning will also be more difficult. Once you get the hang of terrarium gardening you may like to take on this challenge.

closed glass

open glass

bottle glass

Preparing the Soil

A good potting mix is essential for your terrarium. As glass containers don't have drainage you will need a well-aerated, nutritious, springy soil. Using the correct soil mix will also prolong the life of your terrarium.

I recommend using a commercial potting mix from your local nursery or garden centre, as this soil has been sterilised. Preferably, choose a potting mix that does not contain fertiliser, as you don't want to speed up the growth of your plants.

Other types of soil include peat moss, which is rich in organic matter and stores water, and horticultural sand, which is different from beach sand. Horticultural sand is the key drainage ingredient in all soils, providing small pockets that hold air and moisture. You can use perlite instead of sand as this aerates the soil in the same way.

Avoid using soil straight from your garden, as it can retain too much moisture and may contain algae and a menagerie of pests.

- For forest and tropical terrariums, use a regular potting mix or an African Violet mix.
- Desert terrariums prefer a fast-draining, porous potting mix. Use a cactus and succulent mix or a palm and citrus mix.
- Carnivorous plants like acidic, moisture-retentive soil, so a mix of half peat moss and half horticultural grade sand is ideal for these terrariums.

Use caution when working with potting mix. Avoid inhaling or ingesting any particles. Wear gloves and a disposable mask or plant in a well-ventilated area. Wash your hands thoroughly after use.

When adding soil to your terrarium, use a large ladle or if the opening is small, use a funnel to pour your soil into position.

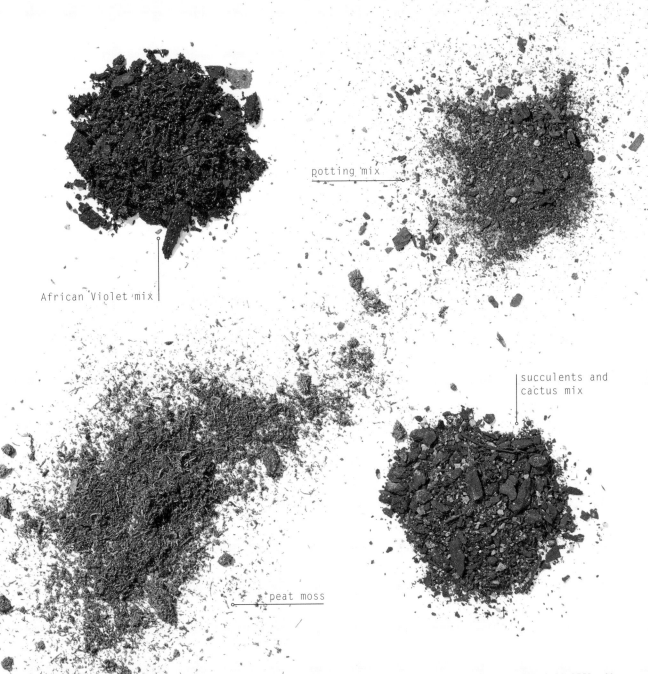

African Violet mix

potting mix

succulents and cactus mix

peat moss

large rocks

river rocks

glass pebbles

gravel

small stones

Rocky Bits

Rocks, pebbles and coarse gravel are essential for the well-being of your terrarium.

Firstly, they form the drainage layer and secondly, they are used to decorate the landscape on top. Rocks and pebbles create contours that look like valleys, rock ledges, hills and cliffs. Adding these scale elements will help your terrarium to look like a scene from nature.

I always try to use three different rock sizes when creating a terrarium. A few larger jagged rocks can be used to emulate boulders; clusters of smooth stones and gravel (or sand) placed at the sides or as dry riverbeds also work really well. I find that placing rocky bits together in clusters looks better than spreading them around and making them look too consistent. When selecting your rocks and pebbles, try to choose a range of colours and sizes.

A variety of pebbles, gravel and rocks can be found at your local nursery, hardware store or even aquarium store. Keep your eye out for interesting feature rocks that you might find in your garden or when you're out walking.

Always rinse and dry your rocky features, to remove any harmful residue and dust.

plants and
decoration

potting mix

horticultural
charcoal

sphagnum moss

separation layer
(optional)

drainage pebbles
or gravel

Layers

As terrariums have no drainage, the layers are important for maintaining a happy garden.

- The bottom layer consists of either small pebbles or gravel. This layer is for drainage and aeration.
- An optional separation layer prevents the soil from dropping down into the drainage layer below. I use a piece of butchers' paper, as it won't interfere with the plants' roots. You could also use fly screen, weed matting or even scrap material. Trace around your container and cut out a shape that is 1 cm (½ in) smaller than the inside of your terrarium. Place the separation layer on top of your bottom layer of pebbles, and add a layer of compacted sphagnum moss tightly around the edge of the glass to prevent any soil from dropping through.
- The third layer is for horticulture charcoal which keeps the soil fresh and odour free. This is the secret ingredient in terrarium gardening. You can find it in garden centres or even in aquarium supply stores.
- The fourth layer is for the potting mix. You need to roughly fill one quarter of the height of your container with soil, remembering to leave enough room for your plants.
- The top layer includes your plants, decorative rocks and pebbles, and any accessories that you want to use.

A long soft paintbrush to help
remove soil from plants.

A wooden skewer for
fine adjustments
in tight spots.

Spoons for adding soil,
charcoal and pebbles,
and for digging holes.

Plastic sauce
bottle for washing
down the sides of
your container
after planting.

Super glue for attaching
figurines to rocks.

Scissors for
pruning and
shaping plants.

Tweezers
for pruning.

A funnel (you can make
one out of rolled-up
paper) for pouring the
soil into position.

Tools

There are a few handy tools that are useful for creating and maintaining your terrarium.

In many instances you should be able to improvise with things you already have in your home. Remember, the smaller the opening of the terrarium the more tools you will need to get inside. So, if you want to keep it simple, make sure you use a container that you can fit your hand inside.

Long-handled tongs for getting into tight spaces.

Small scoop for soil, gravel and pebbles.

A water-spray bottle for watering your plants.

CREATING A GARDEN

Choosing the Right Plants

One of the golden rules of terrarium gardening is to make sure you use compatible plants. It is important to match plants that you would find growing together in nature; for example, you can't mix desert and forest plants together, as they have different needs.

Closed terrariums

These terrariums create a mini ecosystem, which enables the plants to survive for long periods without much care. Moisture is trapped within the terrarium, like an incubator, controlling its atmosphere. The temperature inside is stabilised and protects the terrarium from outside factors, offering the perfect growing conditions for moisture-loving plants. The best plants to use in a closed terrarium are tropical indoor plants with lush green leaves.

Open terrariums

These terrariums are often used for succulents and desert-dwelling plants, as they like lots of ventilation. Unlike sealed terrariums they do not trap moisture and therefore require more watering. These terrariums do not like having wet feet, so you should allow the soil to dry out completely between watering. As well as succulents and cacti, carnivorous plants and air plants also work well in open terrariums. Tropical plants will grow happily but they will need more watering.

Desert

Desert gardens are visually stunning, as arid plants offer a wide range of shapes, colours and textures. In the right conditions desert gardens are hardy and have low water requirements.

Cacti and succulents prefer their environments to be less humid and need adequate air circulation, so open containers are ideal.

Allow your garden to dry out between watering, as these plants require good drainage and don't like their roots to get damp.

Adding interesting rocks and pebbles to a sparsely planted terrarium will help to create a rugged desert-like landscape.

Forest

These terrariums are lush and green, similar to a mini rainforest. Forest plants suit containers that are closed (with a lid) or have a small opening, as they need humid, warm environments to thrive. These conditions are best for ferns, and indoor or tropical plants.

Forest terrariums are very easy to maintain, as they are much more self-sufficient than their desert biome cousins. These are the terrariums you see at your grandma's house or on the internet that have been going for twenty years or more.

Tropical plants are happier in low light, as in nature they would be growing under the rainforest canopy.

Carnivorous

Carnivorous plants are strange and wonderful. They lure insects into their traps by odour and colour, digesting their prey to obtain energy and nutrients.

They are quite unlike any other plants and should be kept separate from other species. They like moist, boggy conditions, but open containers are best, as they allow insects to enter. You can also collect insects to feed your plants: moths, spiders, flies, ants, butterflies, bees and wasps all make a delicious snack. The plants will usually take a few days to digest their prey. Don't use insecticides to kill your insects, as this will affect the plants.

Carnivorous plants require lots of indirect sunlight to survive, so make sure you place your terrarium in a sunny spot. The plants do not like potting mix but prefer a mix of half perlite (or horticulture sand) and half peat moss. They are also quite sensitive to chemicals in tap water, so use distilled or rainwater (where possible) or allow tap water to sit for 12 hours before using.

Carnivorous plants have a dormant period, so don't be alarmed if they die off in winter. Wrap the terrarium in a plastic bag and keep cool over the winter months. Put it in the garage (or fridge if you live in a warm climate), and bring back out to a sunny spot in the spring.

Air Plants

Air plants are unique and fascinating plants that belong to the Bromeliad family.

They require no soil as their nutrients and water are absorbed through their leaves. They use their roots only to anchor themselves to trees and rocks. They require minimal care but they do need air, water and bright indirect light.

The biggest killer for the air plant is not enough water. You will need to immerse your air plant in water for at least 10–20 minutes each week. Shake off any excess water after each soak, and allow your air plant to dry out completely before putting it back into your terrarium; otherwise they are prone to rot. If the leaves curl or roll, then they aren't receiving enough moisture.

After the air plants flower, they will produce little pups that can be propagated to create new plants.

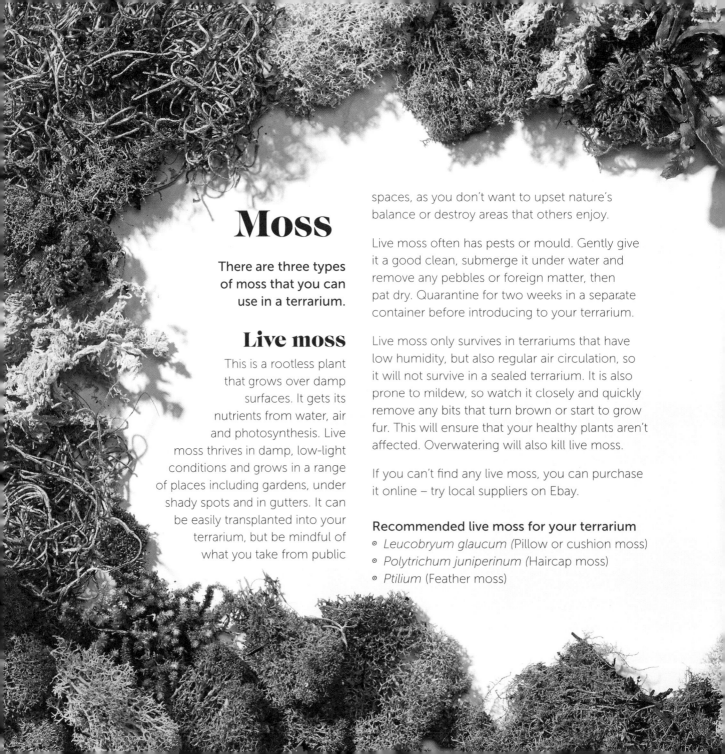

Moss

There are three types of moss that you can use in a terrarium.

Live moss

This is a rootless plant that grows over damp surfaces. It gets its nutrients from water, air and photosynthesis. Live moss thrives in damp, low-light conditions and grows in a range of places including gardens, under shady spots and in gutters. It can be easily transplanted into your terrarium, but be mindful of what you take from public spaces, as you don't want to upset nature's balance or destroy areas that others enjoy.

Live moss often has pests or mould. Gently give it a good clean, submerge it under water and remove any pebbles or foreign matter, then pat dry. Quarantine for two weeks in a separate container before introducing to your terrarium.

Live moss only survives in terrariums that have low humidity, but also regular air circulation, so it will not survive in a sealed terrarium. It is also prone to mildew, so watch it closely and quickly remove any bits that turn brown or start to grow fur. This will ensure that your healthy plants aren't affected. Overwatering will also kill live moss.

If you can't find any live moss, you can purchase it online – try local suppliers on Ebay.

Recommended live moss for your terrarium
- *Leucobryum glaucum (*Pillow or cushion moss)
- *Polytrichum juniperinum (*Haircap moss)
- *Ptilium* (Feather moss)

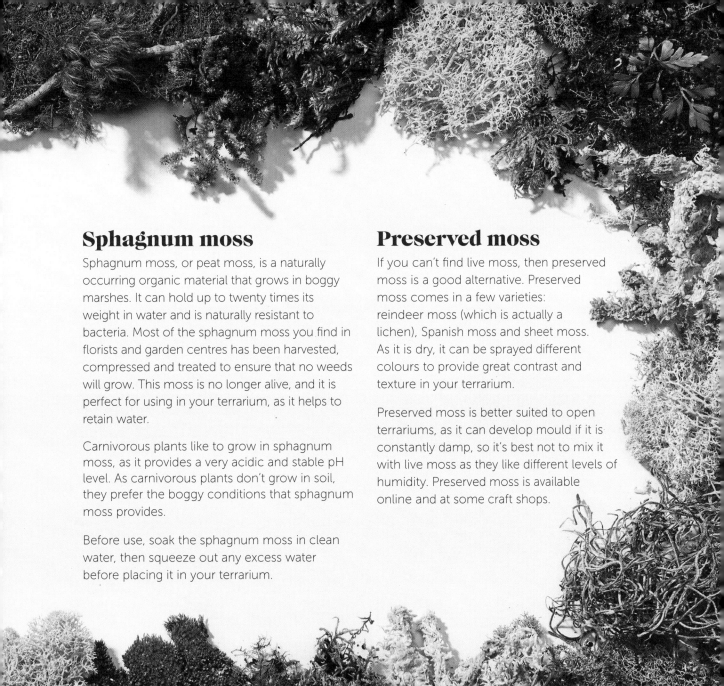

Sphagnum moss

Sphagnum moss, or peat moss, is a naturally occurring organic material that grows in boggy marshes. It can hold up to twenty times its weight in water and is naturally resistant to bacteria. Most of the sphagnum moss you find in florists and garden centres has been harvested, compressed and treated to ensure that no weeds will grow. This moss is no longer alive, and it is perfect for using in your terrarium, as it helps to retain water.

Carnivorous plants like to grow in sphagnum moss, as it provides a very acidic and stable pH level. As carnivorous plants don't grow in soil, they prefer the boggy conditions that sphagnum moss provides.

Before use, soak the sphagnum moss in clean water, then squeeze out any excess water before placing it in your terrarium.

Preserved moss

If you can't find live moss, then preserved moss is a good alternative. Preserved moss comes in a few varieties: reindeer moss (which is actually a lichen), Spanish moss and sheet moss. As it is dry, it can be sprayed different colours to provide great contrast and texture in your terrarium.

Preserved moss is better suited to open terrariums, as it can develop mould if it is constantly damp, so it's best not to mix it with live moss as they like different levels of humidity. Preserved moss is available online and at some craft shops.

THE
PLANTS

Terrarium Plants

There are so many amazing plants you can use in terrarium gardening. Here, I have listed some of my favourites that you should be able to find at your local nursery or garden centre. You may be limited by what is available as some plants may be seasonal or available at different times of the year. The cacti/succulents and the indoor plants/fern areas are good places to start. Some big nurseries will even have their own terrarium section, where you can find small plant varieties perfect for your miniature garden.

Before purchasing, inspect each plant carefully, choosing the healthiest plant on offer and one that is free from pests and dead leaves. As space is limited inside terrariums, look out for dwarf varieties of plants – these will often have 'Nana' in their name.

Group your chosen plants together to check you are happy with the composition. Aim for a variety of colours, heights and textures.

The plants on the following pages are grouped according to terrarium type and growing compatability. Keeping compatible plants together will minimise terrarium heartache. Be prepared to learn through trial and error, as some plants may thrive while others may perish.

Desert plants

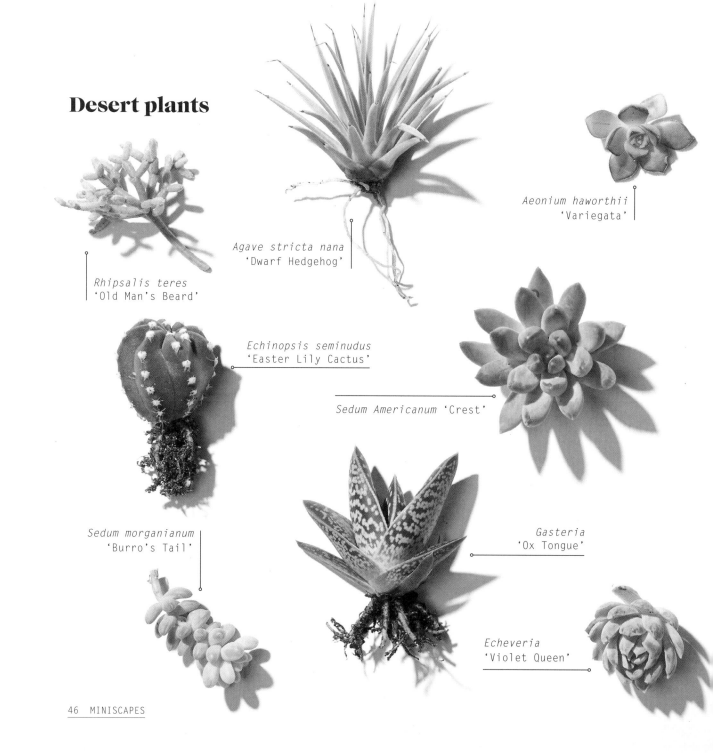

Rhipsalis teres
'Old Man's Beard'

Agave stricta nana
'Dwarf Hedgehog'

Aeonium haworthii
'Variegata'

Echinopsis seminudus
'Easter Lily Cactus'

Sedum Americanum 'Crest'

Sedum morganianum
'Burro's Tail'

Gasteria
'Ox Tongue'

Echeveria
'Violet Queen'

Senecio rowleyanus
'String of Pearls'

Sedum adolphii 'Golden Sedum'

Aeonium lindleyi

Pilosocereus azureus
'Columnar Cactus'

Sedeveria hybrid

Gymnocalycium mihanovichii
friedrichii 'Moon Cactus'

Sedum rubrotinctum
'Jelly Bean'

Desert plants

Graptoveria
'Opalina'

Aylostera deminuta
'Crimson Crown Cactus'

Echeveria
'Emerald Ripple'

Pleiospilos nelii
'Split Rock'

Sedum clavatum
'Stonecrop'

Haworthia fasciata
'Zebra Plant'

Pachyphytum compactum
'Glaucum'

Kalanchoe pumila
'Flower Dust Plant'

Haworthia cooperi

Crassula ovata
'Jade Plant'

Orostachys macrophylla
'Dunce's Cap'

Sedum spathulifolium
'Cape Blanco'

Sedum rubrotinctum var roseum
'Jelly Bean'

Pachyphytum compactum
'Rose'

Tropical plants

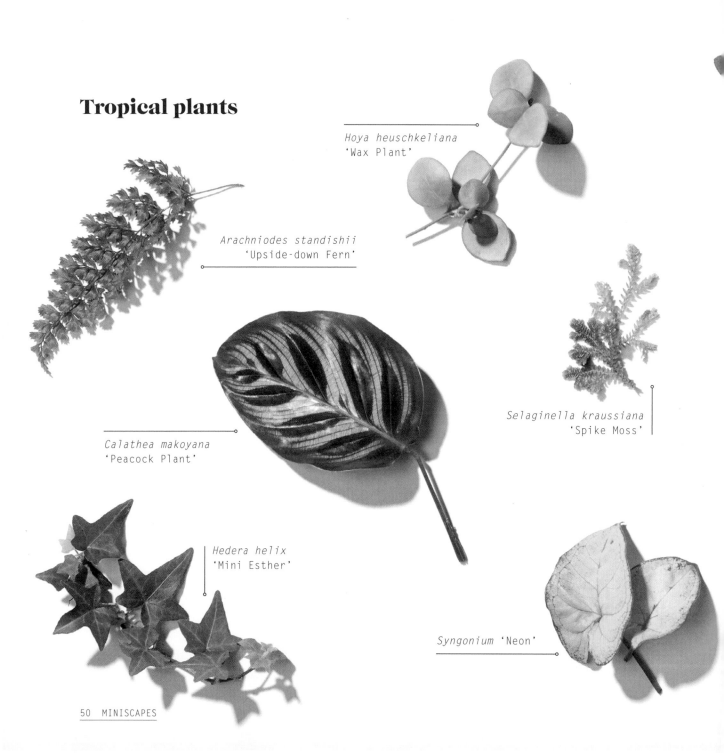

Hoya heuschkeliana
'Wax Plant'

Arachniodes standishii
'Upside-down Fern'

Calathea makoyana
'Peacock Plant'

Selaginella kraussiana
'Spike Moss'

Hedera helix
'Mini Esther'

Syngonium 'Neon'

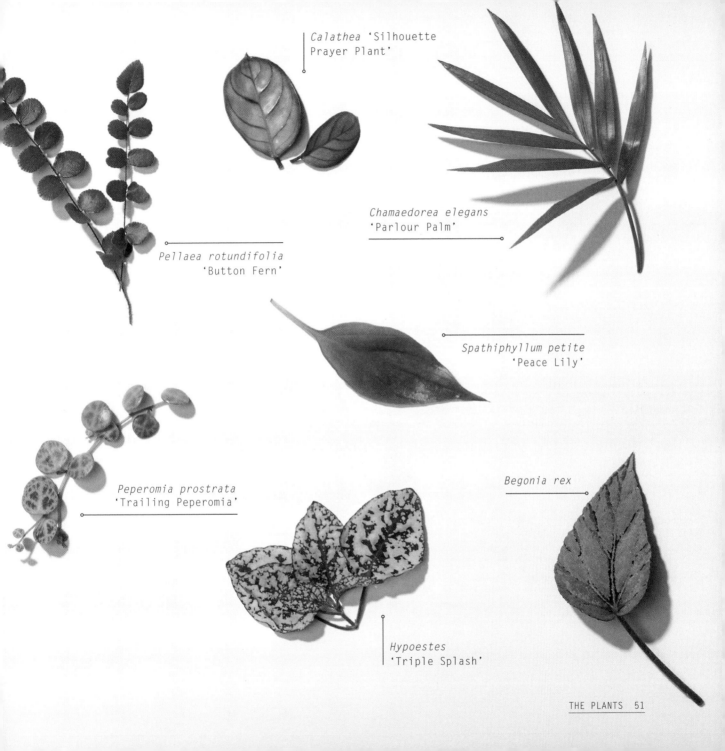

Calathea 'Silhouette Prayer Plant'

Chamaedorea elegans 'Parlour Palm'

Pellaea rotundifolia 'Button Fern'

Spathiphyllum petite 'Peace Lily'

Peperomia prostrata 'Trailing Peperomia'

Begonia rex

Hypoestes 'Triple Splash'

Tropical plants

Schefflera arboricola
'Dwarf Umbrella'

Nephrolepis cordifolia
'Duffii Fern'

Peperomia marmorata
× metallica 'Eden Rosso'

Peperomia hybrid

Pilea cadierei
'Aluminium Plant'

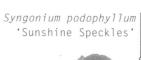

Ficus microcarpa
retusa 'Pot Belly Fig'

Syngonium podophyllum
'Sunshine Speckles'

Humata tyermanii
'White Rabbit's Foot'

Saintpaulia ionantha
'African Violet'

Radermachera sinica
'Asian Bell or China Doll'

Syngonium podophyllum
'Neon'

Peperomia marmorata
'Silver Heart'

Fittonia argyroneura
'Nerve Plant'

Ficus pumila
'Creeping Fig'

Air plants

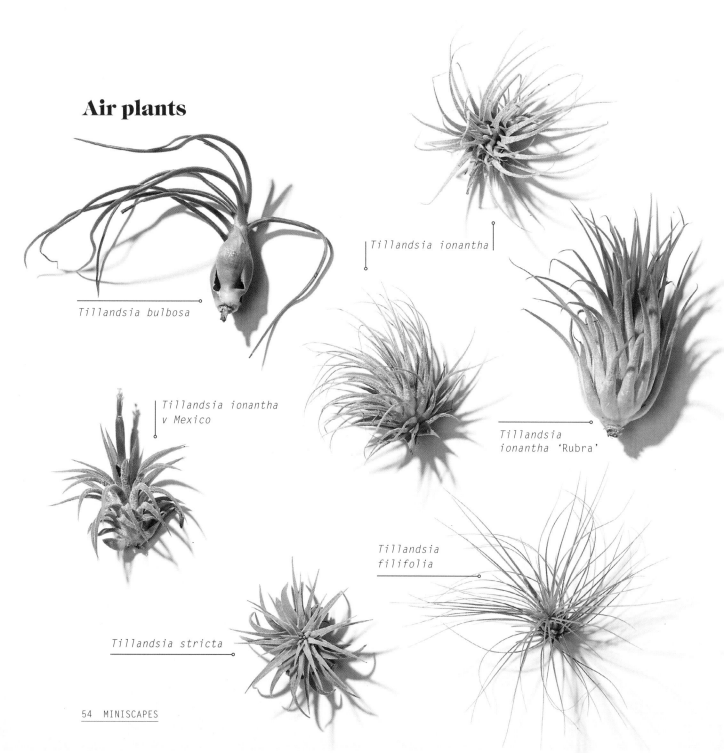

Tillandsia bulbosa

Tillandsia ionantha

Tillandsia ionantha v Mexico

Tillandsia ionantha 'Rubra'

Tillandsia filifolia

Tillandsia stricta

Carnivorous plants

Sarracenia purpurea
'Purple Pitcher Plant'

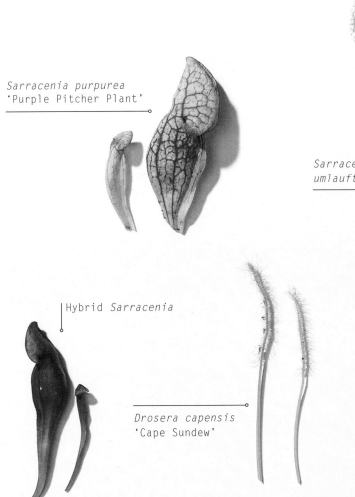

*Sarracenia x
umlauftiana*

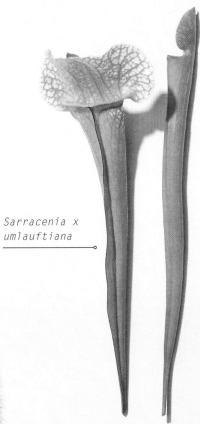

Hybrid *Sarracenia*

Drosera capensis
'Cape Sundew'

Dionaea muscipula
'Venus Fly Trap'

stem cuttings

Propagating Plants

One of the great things about many terrarium plants is that you can easily propagate them in your home from cuttings.

Plants have an amazing ability to duplicate themselves, and by taking a stem or even just a leaf, you can create a whole new plant. Finding plants that are small enough for terrariums can sometimes be challenging and expensive, so growing your own opens up a whole range of leafy options.

I have simplified the instructions for propagating individual plants as much as I can; I could write a whole book on just this topic! There is also lots of information online if you'd like to explore propagation further.

Tropical house plants

STEM CUTTINGS

Choose a healthy non-flowering shoot and make a cut, about 10 cm (4 in) in length, just above a branch node (where the leaf emerges), leaving behind a few leaves. Take the cuttings from the top of your plants where growth is most active. Put the cuttings straight into pre-moistened soil or water. You can also dip your cuttings into rooting hormone powder if you'd like to speed up the process. Roots should start to appear after 7–14 days. Store in a warm, sunny spot with indirect light.

LEAF CUTTINGS

This technique is good for plants with fleshy leaves. Snip off healthy leaves close to the stem of your plant and bury the cut ends of the leaves into some potting mix. You can use a container with a clear lid or even place the pot into a clear plastic bag to increase humidity and create a mini greenhouse.

The best time to take cuttings is in spring and early summer. Keep the soil fairly damp and out of direct sunlight. Vermiculite or a well-draining potting mix are excellent soil types for leaf cuttings.

It can take up to eight weeks for tiny leaves to grow and for new plants to develop. Carefully remove and discard the original leaves and place your new plants into your terrarium.

Succulents

STEM CUTTINGS

It is super easy to propagate your favourite succulent. Using scissors or a sharp knife, cut off a 5 cm (2 in) piece of stem with a few leaves attached from the parent plant. Remove the bottom leaves. Allow a few days for the succulent to dry out and for its 'wound' to heal, before putting into water or directly into soil. After two weeks you should notice roots forming. Transfer your cuttings into potting mix, water and place in a sunny spot. After one month the roots should be established and your succulents will be ready to plant into your terrarium.

LEAF CUTTINGS

The other easy way to propagate succulents is to use their leaves. Remove a few leaves from the parent plant, making a clean cut close to the stem. Again, allow a few days for the end of each leaf to dry out. Arrange the leaves in a tray of potting mix. Water and leave in a sunny spot. After a few weeks the leaves will develop tiny new leaves and roots. Discard the original leaves and transplant into a bigger pot or directly into your terrarium.

ASSEMBLING YOUR TERRARIUM

Building your Miniscape

The process for planting a desert or forest terrarium is generally the same. Ensure that all of your elements are ready to go before starting.

It is important to give yourself enough time. Assembling a terrarium can take anywhere between 20 minutes and 2 hours depending on the complexity of your project.

Always make sure that you thoroughly wash, clean and dry your glass container before starting. Lay out your equipment and inspect your plants – they should look healthy and free from any dead leaves and pests. If you like, you can arrange your plants in the order you would like to plant them. Once you're happy with the layout, you are ready to begin!

The step-by-step instructions in this chapter illustrate the basic steps in terrarium gardening, and can be adapted to any of the projects in this book.

1

Start with a clean glass container.

Add a separation layer (optional). Cut out a piece of butchers' paper that is slightly smaller than the inside of your container. Place this paper on top of the gravel or pebbles.

3

2

Spread crushed gravel or pebbles on the base of your terrarium, so that they fill about ⅕ of the height of your container.

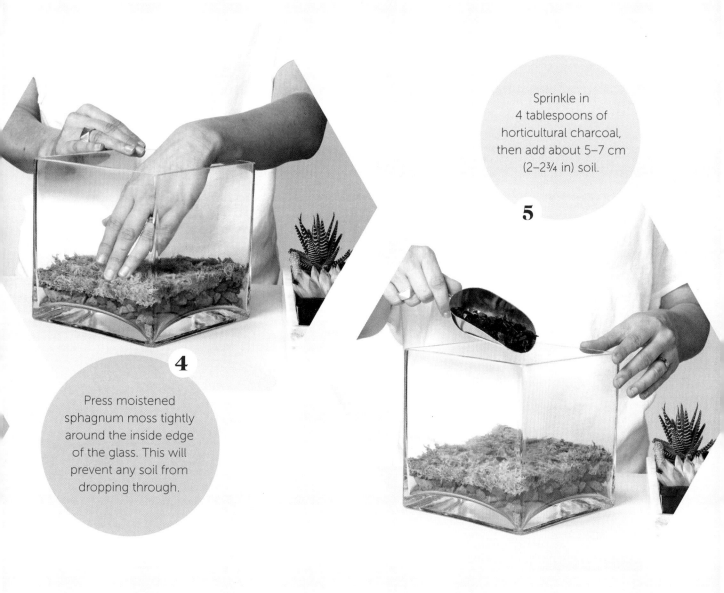

4

Press moistened sphagnum moss tightly around the inside edge of the glass. This will prevent any soil from dropping through.

5

Sprinkle in 4 tablespoons of horticultural charcoal, then add about 5–7 cm (2–2¾ in) soil.

Add more soil in some areas to give you a hill and variations in height.

6

7

Remove the plants from their pots by squeezing the pots and gently pulling the neck of the plant. Crumble away any excess soil from the root ball and trim any roots that are longer than 5 cm (2 in).

8

Dig little pockets in the soil for inserting the plants. Place the plant roots into the hole, and firmly fill in with soil, ensuring that there are no air gaps. Place taller or larger-leafed plants towards the back, and smaller or ground cover plants at the front.

10

Use a water-spray bottle to wash down the sides of your container. Water each plant thoroughly.

9

Finish by adding feature rocks, decorative stones, pebbles, crystals or figurines to give your terrarium an interesting landscape.

LOOKING AFTER YOUR TERRARIUM

Watering

It can be hard to give a predictable schedule for watering your mini garden, as the type of terrarium, season, temperature and amount of available sunlight all affect how much moisture is required. When in doubt, feel the soil — if it's dry, add water; if it's moist, go without. Remember to check your terrarium weekly, as conditions can quickly change.

Overwatering is the biggest threat to terrariums. Too much water can turn your soil soggy and this can be hard to correct as terrariums have no drainage. Water should never rise above the bottom drainage layer.

Whenever possible, use filtered water, or allow tap water to sit for 12 hours before using. Tap water contains salts and minerals that can build up in your terrarium over time.

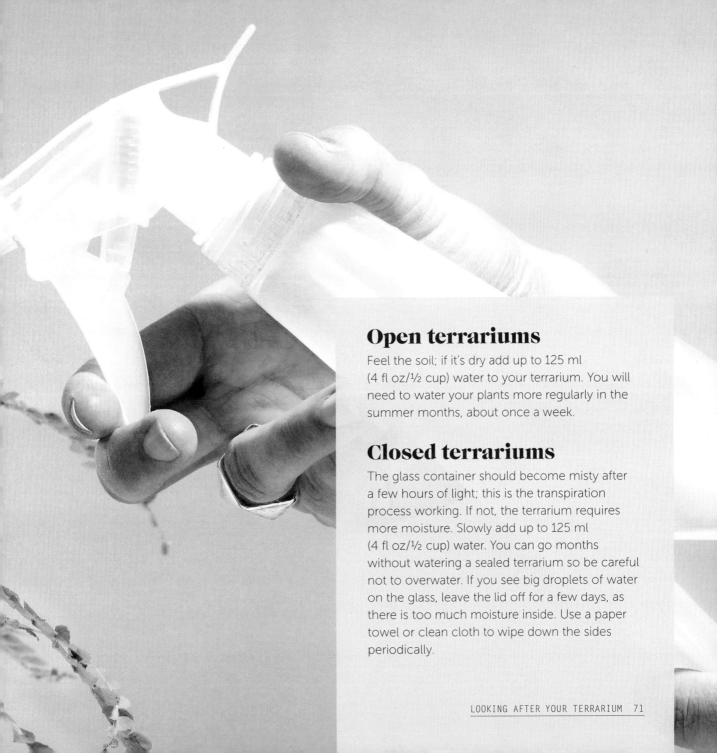

Open terrariums

Feel the soil; if it's dry add up to 125 ml
(4 fl oz/½ cup) water to your terrarium. You will
need to water your plants more regularly in the
summer months, about once a week.

Closed terrariums

The glass container should become misty after
a few hours of light; this is the transpiration
process working. If not, the terrarium requires
more moisture. Slowly add up to 125 ml
(4 fl oz/½ cup) water. You can go months
without watering a sealed terrarium so be careful
not to overwater. If you see big droplets of water
on the glass, leave the lid off for a few days, as
there is too much moisture inside. Use a paper
towel or clean cloth to wipe down the sides
periodically.

Light

Plants will require 6–8 hours of light per day.

Terrariums prefer indirect sunlight, and a southern-facing window is recommended as it provides bright light but not direct sun. Keep your terrarium away from the window, so the sun doesn't directly shine on it. Avoid harsh afternoon direct sunlight and never put your terrarium outside, as the glass will magnify the sun and burn your plants. If you notice your plants reaching to one side, rotate your terrarium periodically, so your plants receive an even distribution of light.

Terrariums also perform quite well under fluorescent or LED light. If your terrarium is in artificial light, make sure it has some periods of darkness, so your plants can rest.

Desert terrariums and plants with more colour in their foliage like lots of bright, indirect light, while forest terrariums can tolerate lower light conditions.

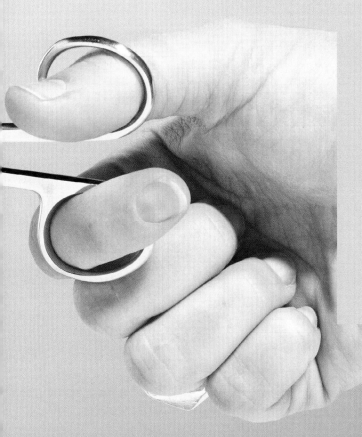

Pruning

As there is not much room in a terrarium, you will need to prune your plants periodically to prevent larger plants taking over and blocking the light needed by smaller plants. You can either use scissors or pinch off any new growth with your fingers. Remember, cuttings can be re-potted to create new plants for other terrariums. If one plant is getting too big, carefully remove it and plant it elsewhere.

You might find that some plants fare better than others – as in nature, it's survival of the fittest. Don't be afraid to be ruthless. Prune back any leaves that touch the side of a sealed container, as the moisture often causes the leaves to rot from being continually wet. Also, remove any plants that die, as rot and mould can quickly spread in a terrarium.

You may notice that some plants become root-bound after a year or so. If this happens, carefully remove the plant and trim back the roots, or replant the whole terrarium to keep it looking fresh.

Pests

Occasionally, you may notice pests lurking inside your terrarium. These may have been present in the potting mix or introduced by moss or other plants.

Symptom	Cause	Treatment
◦ White cotton-like clumps on leaf junctions.	◦ Mealy bugs.	◦ Dab with a cotton bud dipped in rubbing alcohol or use pyrethrum spray (a non-toxic insect killer available from most supermarkets). Remove the plant if the condition doesn't improve.
◦ Sticky, shiny spots. ◦ Yellowing leaves.	◦ Aphids – small insects typically found in clusters under and around stems and leaves. These suck on plant tissue, stunt growth and may eventually kill the plant.	◦ Use pyrethrum spray or remove the infested plant.
◦ Leaves appear pale and washed out. ◦ Fine white webbing. ◦ Yellow blotches on leaves.	◦ Spider mites – adults are brown in colour, oval-shaped, and very tiny (almost too small to see). A sap-sucking pest, which attacks the undersides of leaves.	◦ Wash leaves with insecticidal soap, pyrethrum spray or rubbing alcohol. ◦ Remove the plant if conditions don't improve.

Symptom	Cause	Treatment
◦ Wilting new shoots. ◦ Rice-sized larvae on the undersides of leaves.	◦ White fly – tiny white moths that typically feed on the undersides of leaves, weakening the plant.	◦ Spray the undersides of leaves with insecticidal soap; be sure to spray all the larvae too.
◦ Small black flying bugs.	◦ Fungus gnats – harmless but annoying, these insects are attracted to indoor plants and moist soil.	◦ Firstly, allow the soil to dry out completely for a few days; this will make your soil less appealing to the bugs. ◦ Sprinkle a tablespoon of cinnamon (a natural fungicide) over the soil or spray the inside of your terrarium with pyrethrum spray.
◦ Areas of eaten foliage or missing leaves.	◦ Caterpillars – often nocturnal, these voracious feeders will feed at night and hide during the day.	◦ Act quickly to minimise damage. Inspect your terrarium and remove the caterpillars. If you can't locate them, spray the inside of your terrarium with pyrethrum spray.

Hints and Tips

Regularly observe your terrarium for signs of pests or illness.
If your plants look unwell, firstly make sure that the roots are firmly
covered in soil, allowing moisture to reach each plant. If this doesn't solve
the issue, here are a few other hints and tips to help fix a sickly terrarium.

Symptom	Cause	Treatment
◦ Overgrown.	◦ Planted for a number of years.	◦ Gently remove all the plants, trim them, and separate and salvage what you can. Empty and clean the container and start again.
◦ Leggy or reaching plants.	◦ Not enough light.	◦ Trim the plants and move closer to a light source.
◦ Mould or fungus.	◦ Not enough light. ◦ Too much humidity.	◦ Remove the affected plant or scrape out the mould or fungus.
◦ Yellowing leaves falling off the plant.	◦ Too much moisture. ◦ Inadequate light.	◦ Reduce water intake or take off the lid for a few days if using a closed terrarium. ◦ Move to a sunnier area. ◦ Remove the affected plant.
◦ Limp leaves.	◦ Not planted properly. ◦ Not enough light.	◦ The soil should firmly cover all the roots and there should not be any air pockets. This allows the plant to absorb more water. ◦ Move to a sunnier area.

Symptom	Cause	Treatment
• Salt deposits on glass.	• Tap water.	• Allow water to sit for 12 hours before watering, or use filtered water.
• Crisp and dry leaves.	• Not enough moisture. • Not planted properly.	• Add 125 ml (4 fl oz/½ cup) water. • Ensure that the soil is firmly covering the roots.
• Algae on glass.	• Build up from humidity.	• Wipe down the glass periodically with paper towel or a clean cloth. Don't use any cleaning products on the inside of the glass.
• Mushrooms.	• Bacteria in soil. • Not enough charcoal.	• If the plants are healthy, remove them and wash off any soil from the roots. Empty the terrarium and sterilise it before replanting with fresh soil.
• Wilting leaves, burn spots.	• Too much direct sunlight.	• Move to an area with indirect sunlight.
• White mould on pebbles.	• Purchased pebbles may be coated to make them shiny.	• Remove the affected pebbles and give them a good scrub.
• Sticky brown spots found on the stems and undersides of leaves.	• Scale.	• Swab the affected areas with a cotton bud dipped in rubbing alcohol.
• Musty odour.	• Not enough charcoal.	• Add some extra horticultural charcoal to the surface of your terrarium.

PIMP YOUR TERRARIUM

Decorations

Although terrarium landscapes are beautiful on their own, there are endless decorations you can add to personalise your miniscape; you are only limited by your imagination! Choose items that are made out of hardy materials such as plastic, stone or glass, as porous and spongy items are prone to rot.

Choose a theme and stick to it. Themes not only help you decide which plants to place together, they also add some fun to your terrarium. Figurines, crystals, shells and bones are all great additions to any mini garden.

I would use restraint when adding extras to your terrarium. You don't want it to become too kitsch and distract from the beauty of the landscape. Objects that are slightly hidden from view add an element of surprise for your viewers. Remember, less is more!

Figurines

I love using miniature people and animals to create little scenes within my terrariums. There are so many options available.

You can buy just about anything in model railway miniature form. Look for the HO scale, which has a ratio of 1:87. The little people are 2.5 cm (1 in) high and are the perfect size for your tiny garden. Schleich make a great range of realistic miniature animals. I love hiding their deer, meerkats and bunnies in between plants and behind rocks. You can also find figurines online, in op shops, at markets, or maybe even in your kids' toy box.

Making a fairy garden or dinosaur terrarium with children is a wonderful way to teach them about gardening, while creating a lasting ornament for your child's room. You could add toy dinosaurs, fairies, or tiny mushrooms.

amethyst quartz

agate slice

amethyst quartz

Indian apophyllites

apophyllite cluster

coral quartz

amethyst points
and clear calcite

quartz cluster

green apophyllite

Crystals

Crystals are magnificent additions to any terrarium. They make a lovely alternative to rocks and are an interesting focal point for your garden.

Crystals are traditionally used in healing and meditation, and combining these with natural elements such as plants can produce a very special terrarium. Look for different shapes and colours that complement your plants. Place crystals throughout your landscape or alternatively, use glass pebbles.

Below are a few variations of crystals. You can find these online, or in specialist healing stores.

- Amethyst quartz – lavender to deep violet
- Indian apophyllites – white
- Quartz cluster – crystal cluster
- Green apophyllite – minty green
- Coral quartz – off-white, coral-shaped
- Apophyllite cluster – black stones within a rock
- Agate slice – pink and white rings
- Amethyst points and clear calcite – small purple and white crystal fragments.

Shells

Shells add a lovely beachy feel to your terrarium. They come in an array of sizes and textures, and you can use smaller shells as a substitute for little pebbles.

You can buy shells online or from aquarium stores, and obviously you will find plenty at the beach; just be mindful about taking anything from nature. Mixed shells, coral rubble, sea fans and dried sea urchins all make wonderful additions.

PROJECTS

Let's Begin

It's time to get your hands dirty. You have now learned enough about basic terrarium gardening to create your very own unique and beautiful mini garden.

The following projects are presented in order of difficulty. The simpler projects are great activities to do with children, or you might like to try a few easy terrariums first before tackling anything more complicated.

There's no right way or wrong way to make a terrarium, just see what suits you. Experiment with different plants, decorations and containers and see what happens. You can use these projects as a guide and add your own creative twists to them, or you may want to improvise with plants readily available to you. Either way the diverse range of terrariums in this chapter will inspire you and help take your terrarium gardening to the next level.

Bonsai

This small terrarium is very simple to make and looks great with one feature plant. I've also added a deer figurine to 'roam' the landscape.

BASIC EQUIPMENT

30 cm (12 in) glass vase

1 cup small cream pebbles

brown paper (optional separation layer, see page 25)

1 cup dried sphagnum moss

⅓ cup horticultural charcoal

2 cups potting mix
(or African Violet mix)

PLANTS

1 *Ficus microcarpa retusa*
'Pot Belly Fig'

DECORATIONS

1 lichen-covered branch

1 large rock

small handful of black river pebbles

1 tablespoon horticulture sand

½ cup live moss

1 deer figurine (HO scale) (optional)

small cream pebbles

sphagnum moss

horticultural
charcoal

potting mix

Project steps

1. **Give** the glass a good wash inside and out.

2. **Pour** the cream pebbles into the bottom of the vase, and gently shake to create an even layer. Add a separation layer, if using.

3. **Soak** sphagnum moss in water for a few seconds, then squeeze out the excess water and place a thin layer firmly on top of the pebbles or separation layer. Sprinkle the charcoal evenly over the sphagnum moss.

4. **Add** half of the potting mix to the container, creating different height levels.

5. **Remove** the Pot Belly Fig from its pot and gently scrape away any excess soil from the roots.

6. **Place** the plant inside the vase. Gently press the roots down into the soil and add the remaining soil to cover the roots. The tap roots can sit above the soil.

7. **Add** the branch, large rock, black river pebbles, sand and the deer, if using. Place small clumps of moss between the rocks.

8. **Water** the plants thoroughly with a water-spray bottle.

lichen-covered
branch

large rock

black river
pebbles

live moss

horticultural
sand

*Ficus microcarpa
retusa*

GUIDELINES

☀ Pot belly figs are very
hardy; they can tolerate
bright indirect sunlight
to low-light conditions.

💧 Water regularly. If the
soil is dry, slowly pour
½ cup water into the vase.

💡 You can use any large vase
to make this terrarium.

🖐 Keep the fig leaves
clipped to encourage
a bonsai-tree shape.

Hanging Garden

Hanging terrariums are perfect
for cascading plants, creating a jungle
effect in your living room.

BASIC EQUIPMENT

25 cm (10 in) hanging geometric planter

1 cup small black stones

⅓ cup horticultural charcoal

2 cups potting mix
(or African Violet mix)

PLANTS

1 *Hoya heuschkeliana* 'Wax Plant'

DECORATIONS

1 medium rock

small handful of black river pebbles

¼ cup small grey stones

small black stones

potting mix

horticultural charcoal

Project steps

1. **Give** the glass a good wash inside and out.

2. **Hang** the container or sit it in an empty pot to keep it upright for planting.

3. **Pour** the small black stones into the bottom of the container, and gently shake to create an even layer.

4. **Sprinkle** the charcoal over the stones.

5. **Add** most of the potting mix up to the height of the opening. Dig a hole in the middle of the soil.

6. **Remove** the plant from its pot and gently remove any excess soil from the root ball.

7. **Place** the root ball into the soil hole. Drape the foliage out of the opening.

8. **Add** the remaining soil to cover the roots and press down firmly.

9. **Place** the rock, black river pebbles and small grey stones around the plant to help hold it in place.

10. **Water** the plant thoroughly with a water-spray bottle.

11. **Hang** in position with a wire or rope.

Hoya heuschkeliana

GUIDELINES

☼ Indirect sunlight.

💧 Water regularly. If the soil is dry, slowly pour ½ cup water directly onto the soil. Keep moist in summer.

💡 Don't add too many rocks and pebbles, as it will become too heavy to hang. Cuttings are easy to propagate - just put a stem cutting in water and wait for roots to grow.

🤚 Hoya are very hardy plants with beautiful flowers. Trim off dead flowers after flowering.

black river pebbles

medium rock

small grey stones

Air Capsule

Hang a few of these terrariums together to add an instant pop of green to any room.

BASIC EQUIPMENT

20 cm (8 in) glass capsule

¼ cup small black stones

PLANTS

1 *Tillandsia stricta*

1 *Tillandsia filifolia*

1 *Tillandsia ionantha v Mexico*

DECORATIONS

3 clumps of preserved reindeer moss

2 medium rocks

small
black stones

preserved
reindeer moss

Project steps

1. **Give** the glass capsule a good wash inside and out.

2. **Soak** the air plants in a bowl of water for 30 minutes.

3. **Pour** the stones into the capsule and position the two medium rocks.

4. **Drain** the air plants and shake off any excess water, as they may rot if they hold extra moisture for too long.

5. **Arrange** your air plants in the capsule.

6. **Add** the preserved reindeer moss.

7. **Attach** fishing wire or string to the glass loop at the top of the terrarium, and hang in a sunny spot.

medium rocks

Tillandsia stricta,
Tillandsia filifolia,
Tillandsia ionantha v Mexico

GUIDELINES

Bright, indirect
sunlight.

Remove the plants and soak
in water once a week for
30 minutes. Spritz with
a water-spray bottle in
warmer months.

Air plants do not require
soil; they use their roots
to anchor themselves to
rocks and branches.

Curled leaves indicate
that the plant is not
getting enough water.

Jarred

This project makes use of old kitchen jars. They are perfect for turning into miniature gardens!

BASIC EQUIPMENT

25 cm (10 in) glass canister with lid

1 cup small cream pebbles

brown paper (optional separation layer, see page 25)

1 cup dried sphagnum moss

⅓ cup horticultural charcoal

2 cups potting mix

PLANTS

1 *Ficus benjamina* 'Weeping Fig'

1 *Fittonia verschaffeltii* 'Forest Flame'

1 *Humata tyermanii* 'White Rabbit's Foot'

1 *Selaginella kraussiana* 'Spike Moss'

DECORATIONS

1 medium rock

small handful of river pebbles

¼ cup small black stones

handful of live moss

1 meerkat figurine

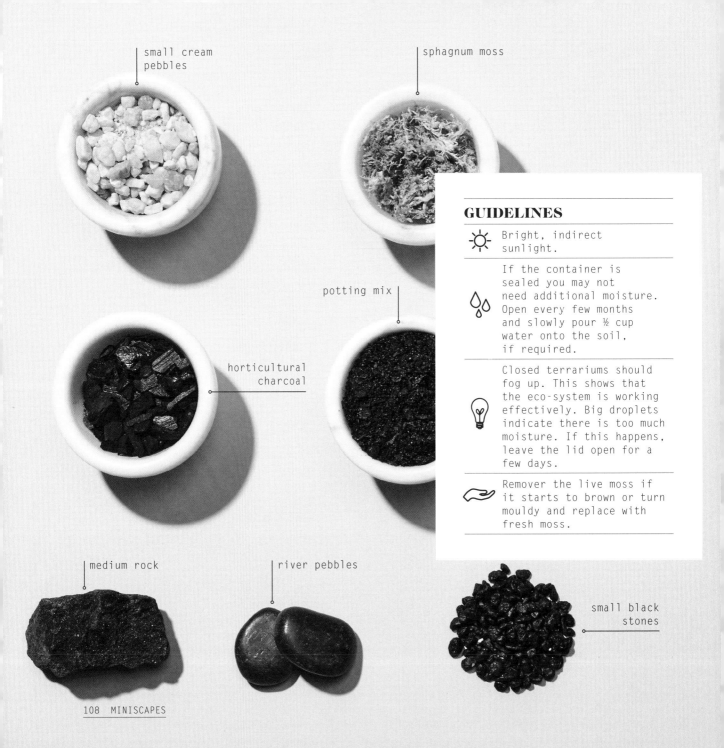

small cream
pebbles

sphagnum moss

potting mix

horticultural
charcoal

GUIDELINES

Bright, indirect
sunlight.

If the container is
sealed you may not
need additional moisture.
Open every few months
and slowly pour ½ cup
water onto the soil,
if required.

Closed terrariums should
fog up. This shows that
the eco-system is working
effectively. Big droplets
indicate there is too much
moisture. If this happens,
leave the lid open for a
few days.

Remover the live moss if
it starts to brown or turn
mouldy and replace with
fresh moss.

medium rock

river pebbles

small black
stones

Ficus benjamina,
Fittonia verschaffeltii,
Humata tyermanii,
Selaginella kraussiana

Project steps

1. **Give** the glass canister a good wash inside and out.

2. **Pour** the small cream pebbles into the bottom of the canister, and gently shake to create an even layer. Add a separation layer, if using.

3. **Soak** the sphagnum moss in water for a few seconds, then squeeze out the excess water and place a thin layer firmly on top of the pebbles or separation layer. You want to form a barrier so that the soil doesn't drop into the drainage layer below.

4. **Sprinkle** the charcoal evenly over the sphagnum moss.

5. **Add** half of the potting mix to the canister, creating different height levels.

6. **Remove** the plants from their pots and gently scrape away any excess soil from the roots.

7. **Arrange** the plants inside the terrarium. Add the remaining soil to cover the roots and press down firmly.

8. **Place** the rock, pebbles and stones in between the plants and position the live moss around the inside edge of the terrarium. Add the meerkat.

9. **Water** the plants thoroughly with a water-spray bottle.

live moss

Minisphere

Tealight orbs are ideal for hanging terrariums. Air plants work particularly well, as they don't require any soil, which can make the terrarium heavy.

BASIC EQUIPMENT

15 cm (6 in) glass tealight orb

¼ cup decorative grey stones

¼ cup glass bead pebbles

PLANTS

1 *Tillandsia stricta*

1 *Tillandsia ionantha* 'Rubra'

1 *Tillandsia ionantha v Mexico*

1 *Tillandsia ionantha* 'Peach'

DECORATIONS

small handful of coral rubble

handful of small shells

1 dried sea urchin

1 dried starfish

glass bead pebbles

decorative grey stones

Tillandsia stricta,
Tillandsia ionantha 'Rubra',
Tillandsia ionantha v Mexico,
Tillandsia ionantha 'Peach'

Project steps

1. **Give** the glass a good wash inside and out.

2. **Soak** the air plants in a bowl of water for 30 minutes.

3. **Pour** the grey stones into the orb.

4. **Add** the glass pebbles around the front of the orb.

5. **Drain** the air plants and shake off any excess water, as they may rot if they hold extra moisture for too long.

6. **Arrange** your air plants in the orb.

7. **Add** the coral, shells, sea urchin and starfish.

8. **Attach** fishing wire or string to the glass loop at the top of the terrarium, and hang in a sunny spot.

GUIDELINES

 Bright, indirect sunlight.

 Remove the plants and soak in water once a week for 30 minutes. Spritz with a water-spray bottle in warmer months.

 Air plants do not require soil; they use their roots to anchor themselves to rocks and branches.

 Curled leaves indicate that the plants are not getting enough water.

small shells

dried sea urchin and starfish

coral rubble

Bubble Bowl

Grouping plants in the middle of a terrarium gives a dynamic effect, and enables you to create interesting landscape features around the inside edge.

BASIC EQUIPMENT

30 cm (12 in) bubble bowl

2 cups small black stones

⅓ cup horticultural charcoal

2 cups potting mix
(or African Violet mix)

PLANTS

1 *Begonia rex*

1 *Spathiphyllum petite* 'Peace Lily'

1 *Soleirolia soleirolii* 'Baby's Tears'

1 *Peperomia marmorata × metallica*
'Eden Rosso'

1 *Fittonia verschaffeltii* 'Forest Flame'

DECORATIONS

1 medium rock

small handful of black river pebbles

¼ cup small grey stones

Project steps

1. **Give** the glass a good wash inside and out.

2. **Pour** the black stones into the bottom of the bowl and gently shake to create an even layer.

3. **Sprinkle** the charcoal evenly over the pebbles.

4. **Add** three quarters of the potting mix to the bowl and create a mound in the middle.

5. **Remove** the plants from their pots and gently scrape away any excess soil, so you are only left with the root balls.

6. **Place** tall plants in the middle and surround with the smaller plants. Divide up the 'Baby's Tears' and plant around the edge as they make great ground cover. Add the remaining soil to cover the roots and press down firmly around the root balls.

7. **Add** the medium rock, river pebbles and small grey stones.

8. **Water** the plants thoroughly with a water-spray bottle.

Begonia rex,
Spathiphyllum petite,
Soleirolia soleirolii,
Peperomia marmorata
× metallica,
Fittonia verschaffeltii

black river
pebbles

medium rock

small grey
stones

GUIDELINES

 Indirect sunlight.

 Slowly pour 1 cup water
directly onto the soil,
whenever it feels dry.

 Plants with colour in
their foliage require
more light and moisture.

 Turn the terrarium
periodically if the
plants start reaching
to one side.

Dishy

A round open container is perfect for desert landscapes. This terrarium looks great as a centre-piece on any table.

BASIC EQUIPMENT

30 cm (12 in) round glass bowl

4 cups small cream pebbles

½ cup horticultural charcoal

6 cups potting mix (or succulent soil)

PLANTS

3 *Euphorbia tirucalli* 'Sticks on Fire'

2 *Crassula ovata* 'Jade Plant'

2 *Sedum rubrotinctum var. roseum* 'Jelly Bean'

1 *Aeonium lindleyi*

1 *Crassula ovata* 'Gollum'

2 *Aeonium haworthii* 'Variegata'

1 *Sedum clavatum* 'Stonecrop'

1 *Echeveria* 'Violet Queen'

DECORATIONS

4 large rocks

handful of black and brown river pebbles

1 cup black shiny decorative pebbles

small cream pebbles

horticultural charcoal

potting mix

GUIDELINES

☀ Bright, indirect sunlight.

💧 Slowly pour 1 cup water directly onto the soil once a month in winter and every two weeks in summer. Allow the soil to dry out between watering.

💡 Cuttings are great to use in these desert gardens.

🖐 Rotate occasionally if plants start to reach to one side.

Project steps

1. **Give** the glass a good wash inside and out.

2. **Pour** the small cream pebbles into the bottom of the bowl, and gently shake to create an even layer.

3. **Sprinkle** the charcoal evenly over the pebbles.

4. **Add** three quarters of the potting mix.

5. **Remove** the plants from their pots and gently scrape away any excess soil from the root balls.

6. **Dig** small holes in the soil. Place small plants around the edge and tall plants in the middle. Add the remaining soil to cover the roots and press down firmly.

7. **Add** the large rocks, river pebbles and shiny decorative pebbles around the inside edge of the terrarium and in between the plants.

8. **Water** the plants thoroughly with a water-spray bottle.

Euphorbia tirucalli, Crassula ovata, Sedum rubrotinctum, Aeonium lindleyi, Crassula ovata, Aeonium haworthii, Sedum clavatum, Echeveria

black and brown river pebbles

black shiny decorative pebbles

large rocks

Teardrop

You can add figurines to your terrarium to tell a story – here, a woman photographs a rare, but deadly, giant Amazonian killer bunny!

BASIC EQUIPMENT

20 cm (8 in) teardrop vase

2 cups gravel

brown paper (optional separation layer, see page 25)

1 cup dried sphagnum moss

⅓ cup horticultural charcoal

2 cups potting mix (or African Violet mix)

PLANTS

1 *Hedera helix* 'Mini Esther'

1 *Pilea cadierei* 'Aluminium Plant'

1 *Schefflera arboricola* 'Dwarf Umbrella'

1 *Syngonium podophyllum* 'Neon'

DECORATIONS

handful of preserved Spanish moss

1 large rock

handful of black river pebbles

⅓ cup small black stones

1 small lady figurine (HO scale)

1 bunny figurine

superglue

gravel

sphagnum moss

GUIDELINES

 Bright, indirect
sunlight

 Slowy pour ½ cup water
directly onto the soil
once a month in winter and
every two weeks in summer.

potting mix

 Adding preserved Spanish
moss to this terrarium
helps to create a densely
covered garden. In a
closed terrarium this
moss may rot due to
high humidity.

Regularly trim larger
plants, so the foliage
stays within the glass.

horticultural
charcoal

small black
stones

black river
pebbles

large rock

bunny figurine

Hedera helix,
Pilea cadierei,
Schefflera arboricola,
Syngonium podophyllum

Project steps

1. **Give** the glass a good wash inside and out.

2. **Pour** gravel into the bottom of the vase and gently shake to create an even layer. Add a separation layer, if using.

3. **Soak** sphagnum moss in water for a few seconds, then squeeze out the excess water and place a thin layer firmly on top of the pebbles or separation layer. You want to form a barrier so that the soil doesn't drop into the drainage layer below.

4. **Sprinkle** the charcoal evenly over the sphagnum moss.

5. **Add** three quarters of the potting mix to the terrarium, creating a mound in the middle.

6. **Remove** the plants from their pots and gently scrape away any excess soil, so you are only left with the root balls.

7. **Place** the plants in the middle of the terrarium. Add the remaining soil to cover the roots and press down firmly on the root balls.

8. **Position** the preserved Spanish moss in between the plants to create a jungle feel.

9. **Add** the large rock, river pebbles and black stones around the inside edge.

10. **Attach** the figurines to a rock with superglue, then add to the terrarium.

11. **Water** the plants thoroughly with a water-spray bottle.

preserved
Spanish moss

Pitcher Perfect

A large fishbowl is ideal for these carnivorous plants, as you can reach in to feed them the odd insect or two. Kids love helping out with this terrarium!

BASIC EQUIPMENT

35 cm (14 in) glass fishbowl

3 cups gravel

½ cup horticultural charcoal

1 cup peat moss

1 cup horticultural sand

PLANTS

3 *Sarracenia x umlauftiana* 'Pitcher Plant'

DECORATIONS

2 large rocks

handful of black river pebbles

1 cup live moss

gravel

horticultural charcoal

peat moss and horticultural sand

Project steps

1. **Give** the glass a good wash inside and out.

2. **Pour** the gravel into the bottom of the fishbowl, and gently shake to create an even layer.

3. **Sprinkle** the charcoal evenly over the gravel.

4. **Mix** the peat moss and sand together and add half to the fishbowl.

5. **Remove** the plants from their pots and gently scrape away any excess soil from the root balls. Arrange the plants in the centre of the bowl. Add the extra soil to ensure the roots are covered firmly.

6. **Place** the large rocks and black river pebbles in between the plants. Add the live moss around the inside edge of the terrarium.

7. **Water** the plants thoroughly with a water-spray bottle.

Sarracenia x umlauftiana

live moss

GUIDELINES

 Lots of bright, indirect sunlight.

 Carnivorous plants like moist, boggy conditions. Use distilled water or rainwater, if possible, as they are sensitive to the chemicals in tap water. In summer, slowly pour ½ cup water directly onto the soil once a week. Less moisture is required in cooler months.

Pitcher plants will have a dormant period during winter where the leaves will die back. Keep in a cool environment and the leaves will return in spring. Rotate occasionally if the plants start to reach to one side.

Carnivorous plants get their nutrients from capturing and digesting insects, so drop an insect into their traps once a week.

large rocks

black river pebbles

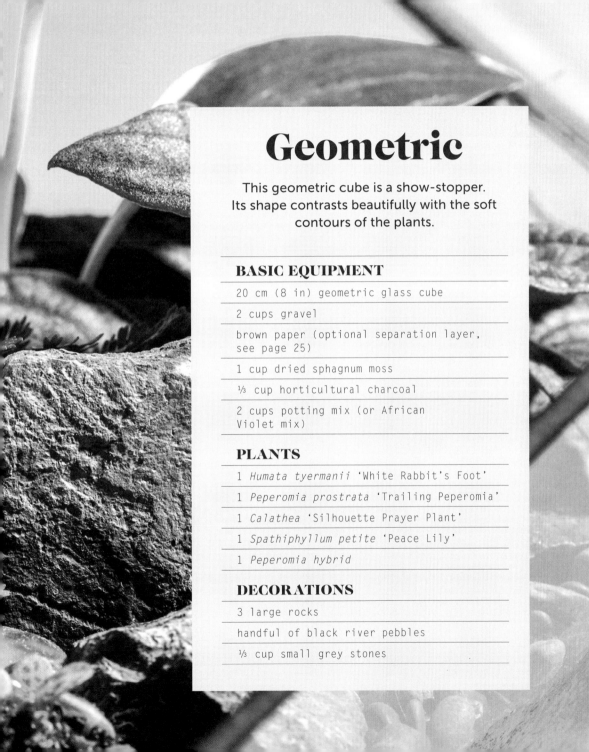

Geometric

This geometric cube is a show-stopper.
Its shape contrasts beautifully with the soft
contours of the plants.

BASIC EQUIPMENT

20 cm (8 in) geometric glass cube

2 cups gravel

brown paper (optional separation layer,
see page 25)

1 cup dried sphagnum moss

⅓ cup horticultural charcoal

2 cups potting mix (or African
Violet mix)

PLANTS

1 *Humata tyermanii* 'White Rabbit's Foot'

1 *Peperomia prostrata* 'Trailing Peperomia'

1 *Calathea* 'Silhouette Prayer Plant'

1 *Spathiphyllum petite* 'Peace Lily'

1 *Peperomia hybrid*

DECORATIONS

3 large rocks

handful of black river pebbles

⅓ cup small grey stones

gravel

sphagnum moss

horticultural
charcoal

potting mix

large rocks and
river pebbles

small grey
stones

Project steps

1. **Give** the glass a good wash inside and out.

2. **Pour** the gravel into the bottom of the cube. Add a separation layer, if using.

3. **Soak** the sphagnum moss in water for a few seconds, then squeeze out the excess water and place a thin layer firmly on top of the gravel or separation layer. You want to form a barrier so that the soil doesn't drop into the drainage layer below.

4. **Sprinkle** the charcoal evenly over the sphagnum moss.

5. **Add** three quarters of the potting mix to the container and create a mound in the middle.

6. **Remove** the plants from their pots and gently scrape away any excess soil, so you are only left with the root balls.

7. **Place** taller plants towards the back of the terrarium and smaller plants at the front. Add the remaining soil to cover the roots and press down firmly.

8. **Add** the large rocks, river pebbles and small grey stones.

9. **Water** the plants thoroughly with a water-spray bottle.

*Humata tyermanii,
Peperomia prostrata,
Calathea, Spathiphyllum
petite, Peperomia hybrid*

GUIDELINES

 Indirect sunlight.

 This cube has a glass door. When the door is closed it will require little watering. If left open, water regularly and don't allow the soil to dry out.

 Geometric glass cubes can be purchased from Ebay and Etsy.

 If the door is closed, the inside of the glass may need wiping down with paper towel periodically.

Prickly Pear

This terrarium is a cacti paradise!
The tall vessel helps to protect little
fingers from the spiky leaves.

BASIC EQUIPMENT

35 cm (14 in) pear-shaped glass container

3 cups small black stones

½ cup horticultural charcoal

4 cups potting mix (or succulent soil)

PLANTS

1 *Gymnocalycium mihanovichii friedrichii*
'Moon Cactus'

1 *Haworthia fasciata* 'Zebra Plant'

1 *Pilosocereus azureus* 'Columnar Cactus'

1 *Aloe longistyla*

3 *Lobivia silvestrii* 'Peanut Cactus'

2 *Echeveria glauca*

1 *Rhipsalidopsis gaertneri*
'Easter Cactus'

DECORATIONS

5 large rocks

handful of black river pebbles

¼ cup cream gravel

¼ cup light grey pebbles

¼ cup dark grey stones

small black stones

horticultural charcoal

potting mix

Project steps

1. **Give** the glass a good wash inside and out.

2. **Pour** the black stones into the bottom of the bowl and gently shake to create an even layer.

3. **Sprinkle** the charcoal evenly over the stones.

4. **Add** three quarters of the potting mix to the container.

5. **Remove** the plants from their pots and gently scrape away any excess soil, so you are only left with the root balls.

6. **Place** small plants around the inside edge of the terrarium and tall plants in the middle. Add the remaining soil to cover the roots and press down firmly around the root balls.

7. **Place** the large rocks and river pebbles in between the plants.

8. **Add** a section of cream gravel. Then add an area of grey pebbles and dark grey stones.

9. **Water** the plants thoroughly with a water-spray bottle.

Gymnocalycium mihanovichii friedrichii, Haworthia fasciata, Pilosocereus azureus, Aloe longistyla, Lobivia silvestrii, Echeveria glauca, Rhipsalidopsis gaertneri

light grey pebbles

cream gravel

black river pebbles

large rocks

dark grey stones

Crystal Palace

Crystals are a great addition to desert terrariums, as their colours complement many succulents and cacti. Together, they create a magical zen garden.

BASIC EQUIPMENT

30 cm (12 in) round glass bowl

4 cups small black stones

½ cup horticultural charcoal

6 cups potting mix (or succulent soil)

PLANTS

1 *Agave stricta nana* 'Dwarf Hedgehog'

2 *Echeveria* 'Violet Queen'

2 *Graptoveria* 'Opalina'

1 *Sedum spathulifolium* 'Cape Blanco'

1 *Pachyphytum compactum* 'Glaucum'

1 *Senecio* 'Blue Chalk Sticks'

DECORATIONS

3 amethyst quartz crystals

handful of amethyst points

handful of clear calcite chips

1 cup clear glass pebbles

1 cup horticultural sand

small black stones   horticultural charcoal   potting mix

Project steps

1. **Give** the glass a good wash inside and out.

2. **Pour** the small black stones into the bottom of the bowl and gently shake to create an even layer.

3. **Spread** the charcoal evenly over the stones.

4. **Add** three quarters of the potting mix to the container and spread out evenly.

5. **Remove** the plants from their pots and gently scrape away any excess soil, so you are only left with the root balls.

6. **Arrange** your plants in the terrarium. Add the remaining soil to cover the roots and press down firmly on the root balls.

7. **Add** the crystals, and then add the glass pebbles and horticultural sand around the inside edge of the terrarium.

8. **Water** the plants thoroughly with a water-spray bottle.

amethyst quartz crystals

clear calcite chips

amethyst points

clear glass pebbles

horticultural sand

GUIDELINES

 Bright, indirect sunlight.

 Slowy pour 1 cup water directly onto the soil once a month in winter and every two weeks in summer. Allow the soil to dry out between watering.

 Aim to keep the colour palette quite soft and neutral when choosing your plants. This will complement the colour of the crystals.

 Remove dead flowers after flowering.

Agave stricta nana,
Echeveria, Graptoveria,
Sedum spathulifolium,
Pachyphytum compactum,
Senecio

Flask Garden

This project makes use of an old laboratory flask – not only does it look great, it's perfect for housing hungry carniverous plants!

BASIC EQUIPMENT

3 litre (101 fl oz) conical flask

1 cup small black stones

brown paper (optional separation layer, see page 25)

1 cup dried sphagnum moss

⅓ cup horticultural charcoal

1 cup peat moss

1 cup horticultural sand

PLANTS

1 *Dionaea muscipula* 'Venus Fly Trap'

1 *Sarracenia* 'Pitcher Plant'

1 Drosera capensis 'Cape Sundew'

DECORATIONS

2 large rocks

½ cup live moss

handful of black river pebbles

small
black stones

peat moss and
horticultural sand

horticultural
charcoal

Project steps

1. **Give** the flask a good wash inside and out.

2. **Pour** small black stones into the bottom of the flask, and gently shake to create an even layer. Add a separation layer, if using.

3. **Soak** sphagnum moss in water for a few seconds, then squeeze out the excess water and place a thin layer firmly on top of the stones or separation layer. You want to form a barrier so that the soil doesn't drop into the drainage layer below.

4. **Sprinkle** the charcoal evenly over the sphagnum moss.

5. **Mix** the peat moss and sand together and add half of this mixture to the flask.

6. **Gently** tap the plants out of their pots. Scrape away any excess soil, so you are left with only the root balls.

7. **Arrange** the plants in the soil. Add the remaining soil to cover the roots and press firmly. Avoid getting soil inside the plants' traps.

8. **Place** the large rocks, live moss and river pebbles in between the plants.

9. **Water** the plants thoroughly with a water-spray bottle.

Dionaea muscipula
Sarracenia
Drosera capensis

sphagnum moss

large rocks

live moss

black river pebbles

GUIDELINES

☼ Lots of bright, indirect sunlight.

💧 A warm humid environment with constant moisture is ideal. Add ½ cup water per week. Use distilled water or rainwater, if possible, as the plants are sensitive to the chemicals in tap water.

💡 Science beakers and flasks are available online in various sizes from education supply stores.

🤚 Carnivorous plants get their nutrients from capturing and digesting insects, so drop an insect into their traps once a week or when possible.

Woody

Sometimes less is more. In this terrarium, a single Parlour Palm reaches up above the pretty ground cover to give a striking effect.

BASIC EQUIPMENT

25 cm (10 in) wood-base terrarium

1 cup small cream pebbles

⅓ cup horticultural charcoal

2 cups potting mix (or African Violet mix)

PLANTS

1 *Chamaedorea elegans* 'Parlour Palm'

1 *Humata tyermanii* 'White Rabbit's Foot'

1 *Fittonia argyroneura* 'Nerve Plant'

1 *Fittonia verschaffeltii* 'Red Star'

DECORATIONS

2 large river rocks

handful of black river pebbles

⅓ cup small black stones

small cream pebbles

horticultural charcoal

potting mix

Project steps

1. **Give** the glass a good wash inside and out.

2. **Pour** the cream pebbles into the bottom of the terrarium, but don't go above the wooden base level, so the drainage layer isn't visible. Gently shake to create an even layer.

3. **Sprinkle** the charcoal over the pebbles.

4. **Add** three quarters of the potting mix and create a mound in the middle.

5. **Remove** the plants from their pots and gently remove any excess soil, so you are only left with the root balls.

6. **Place** the plants inside the terrarium. Gently press the roots down into the soil and add the remaining soil to cover the roots.

7. **Add** the large rocks, river pebbles and black stones around the inside edge of the terrarium.

8. **Water** the plants thoroughly with a water-spray bottle.

black river pebbles

large river rocks

small black stones

GUIDELINES

 Indirect sunlight.

 This terrarium is sealed, so it requires little watering. If you don't see any moisture forming on the inside of the glass, or if the soil is dry to touch, slowly pour ⅓ cup water onto the soil.

 Wipe down the inside of the glass periodically with paper towel.

Sealed terrariums are self sufficient and require little maintenance.

Chamaedorea elegans,
Humata tyermanii,
Fittonia argyroneura,
Fittonia verschaffeltii

She Sells Seashells

Shells and coral give a wonderful beachy effect to a terrarium. You can purchase dried sea materials from your local aquarium store.

BASIC EQUIPMENT

35 cm (14 in) concrete-bottomed hurricane vase

2 cups gravel

½ cup horticultural charcoal

2 cups potting mix (or African Violet mix)

PLANTS

1 *Syngonium* 'Neon'

1 *Hypoestes phyllostachya* 'Pink Polka Dot'

1 *Hypoestes phyllostachya* 'White Polka Dot'

1 *Saintpaulia ionantha* 'African Violet'

DECORATIONS

1 dried sea fan

1 cup grey decorative pebbles

1 cup coral rubble

handful of shells

1 dried sea urchin

1 dried starfish

gravel

shells, dried
starfish and
sea urchin

coral rubble

potting mix

grey decorative
pebbles

horticultural
charcoal

Project steps

1. **Give** the glass a good wash inside and out.

2. **Pour** the gravel into the bottom of the vase, but don't go above the concrete base level, so the drainage layer isn't visible. Gently shake to create an even layer.

3. **Sprinkle** the charcoal evenly over the gravel.

4. **Add** three quarters of the potting mix and create a mound in the middle.

5. **Push** the sea fan into the potting mix at the back of the vase.

6. **Remove** the plants from their pots and gently scrape away any excess soil, so you are only left with the root balls.

7. **Place** the taller plants at the back of the vase and the smaller plants towards the front. Add the remaining soil to firmly cover the roots.

8. **Add** the decorative pebbles and the coral rubble around the inside edge of the vase – try to cover all of the soil. Add the shells, sea urchin and starfish.

9. **Water** the plants thoroughly with a water-spray bottle.

GUIDELINES

 Indirect sunlight.

 Slowly pour ½ cup water directly onto the soil every 7-14 days, depending on the season and climate. Keep the soil moist between watering but not soaking wet.

 Choose plants with white in their foliage to complement the coral and seashells.

 Replace any plants that outgrow their environment.

Syngonium,
Hypoestes phyllostachya,
Hypoestes phyllostachya,
Saintpaulia ionantha

Down to the Woods

This large terrarium uses multiples of
one plant that will, with time, create
a mini forest effect.

BASIC EQUIPMENT

40 cm (16 in) square glass tank

4 cups black river rocks

30 cm (12 in) square piece of butchers'
paper or weed matting (separation layer,
see page 25)

2 cups dried sphagnum moss

½ cup horticultural charcoal

2 cups potting mix
(or African Violet mix)

PLANTS

1 *Radermachera sinica* 'Asian Bell
or China Doll'

DECORATIONS

small handful of black river rocks

¼ cup small black stones

2 large rocks

1 cup live moss

black river
rocks

sphagnum moss

horticultural
charcoal

potting mix

Radermachera sinica

small black
stones

GUIDELINES

☼ Indirect sunlight.

◊◊ Water regularly. If the
soil is dry, slowly pour
1 cup water directly
onto the tree (so it
doesn't disrupt the soil
too much). Keep moist in
summer. Less water is
required in cooler months.

💡 Glass square tanks are
available at most
aquarium stores.

✋ Trim the leaves regularly
to maintain the shape of
each tree.

large rocks

live moss

black river rocks

Project steps

1. **Give** the glass a good wash inside and out.

2. **Place** the river rocks on the bottom of the tank, building them up higher at the sides.

3. **Add** the separation layer. Spray the paper with water to make it malleable.

4. **Soak** sphagnum moss in water for a few seconds, then squeeze out the excess water and create a raised border around the edge of the paper. This will stop the soil dropping into the drainage layer below.

5. **Sprinkle** the charcoal evenly over the sphagnum moss.

6. **Add** two thirds of the potting mix and form a mound in the centre.

7. **Remove** the plant from its pot and gently scrape away any excess soil from the roots. You should have a few plants attached to the root ball; if so, gently separate apart.

8. **Make** holes in the soil and add the plants in a line.

9. **Add** the remaining soil to cover the roots and press down firmly.

10. **Place** a few more river rocks around the edges to hide the separation layer, then decorate with the small black stones, large rocks and live moss.

11. **Water** the plants thoroughly with a water-spray bottle.

Acknowledgements

I would like to thank the following contributors for their generous support in creating this book.

Collectors Corner
www.collectorscorner.com.au
Succulents, cacti, carnivorous, air plants, tropical plants and crystals.

Biemond Nursery
www.biemond.com.au
Indoor, exotic plants and ferns.

Twenty21
www.twenty21.com.au
www.marblebasics.com.au
Beautiful marble vessels used throughout the book from 'Marble Basics'.

Schleich
www.schleich-s.com.au
Realistic range of miniature animals.

Thanks to Jack Hutchings for your love and support; my children Harlan and Ettie for your infectious excitement and sharing my love of miniature things; Helen Cregan for being the best Mum and correcting my bad grammar; David Cregan, Elspeth MacDonald, Felicity Jack, Rob Hutchings and Sue Norman for your constant encouragement; my lovely assistants Ola Roman, Jem Taylor and Melissa D'Alessandro for all your help, and Natalie Turnball for your remote stylist tips; Jeno Kapitany for letting me raid your amazing nursery; Steve Biemond for sending me trays and trays of wonderful plants; Lara Davis and Jess Wright @ Homework Studios for being brilliant studio buddies and putting up with my constant chaos; Melbourne Art Supplies for allowing us to use your space for the photoshoot; Carlo Campora (Twenty21) and Bonnie Adams (Marble Basics) for being so accommodating; Adam Brown (The Agent Group) for helping me source props at the last minute; Jeremy (Jacky Winter Group) and Beci Orpin for your helpful advice; Jess Moore and Simone Hicks for reading all the small print; Kylie Walker-Povey, Mel Yuan, and Melissa Pain for helping me wrangle my kids; Lucy Heaver for making this dream project come to life!; Kate Barraclough and Mark Campbell for designing a book that is both practical and beautiful!; Rich Macdonald for capturing amazing reflection-free photographs – I hope you never have to photograph another terrarium in your life! And finally thanks to Hardie Grant for publishing another great book.

This book is dedicated to Declan.

Published in 2016 by Hardie Grant Books

Hardie Grant Books (Australia)
Ground Floor, Building 1
658 Church Street
Richmond, Victoria 3121
www.hardiegrant.com.au

Hardie Grant Books (UK)
5th & 6th Floors
52–54 Southwark Street
London SE1 1UN
www.hardiegrant.co.uk

A Cataloguing-in-Publication entry is available from the catalogue of the National Library of Australia at www.nla.gov.au

Miniscapes
ISBN: 9781743791400

Publishing Director: Fran Berry
Publisher and Project Editor: Lucy Heaver
Design Manager: Mark Campbell
Designer: Kate Barraclough
Photographer: Rich Macdonald
Production Manager: Todd Rechner

Colour reproduction by Splitting Image Colour Studio
Printed and bound in China by 1010 Printing International Limited

JANUARY 2017